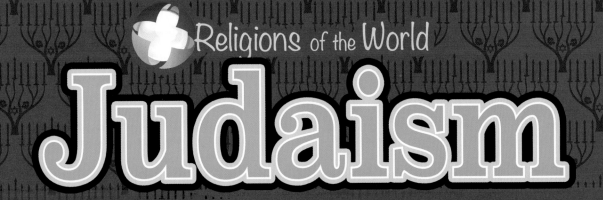

Religions of the World

Judaism

Rita Faelli

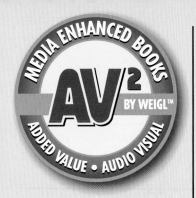

AV² provides enriched content that supplements and complements this book. Weigl's AV² books strive to create inspired learning and engage young minds in a total learning experience.

Your AV² Media Enhanced books come alive with...

 Audio
Listen to sections of the book read aloud.

 Key Words
Study vocabulary, and complete a matching word activity.

 Video
Watch informative video clips.

 Quizzes
Test your knowledge.

Go to **www.av2books.com**, and enter this book's unique code.

BOOK CODE

F 6 7 3 3 2 4

 Embedded Weblinks
Gain additional information for research.

 Slide Show
View images and captions, and prepare a presentation.

AV² by Weigl brings you media enhanced books that support active learning.

 Try This!
Complete activities and hands-on experiments.

... and much, much more!

Published by AV² by Weigl
350 5th Avenue, 59th Floor
New York, NY 10118
Website: www.av2books.com

Library of Congress Control Number: 2015942088

ISBN 978-1-4896-4039-0 (hardcover)
ISBN 978-1-4896-4040-6 (soft cover)
ISBN 978-1-4896-4041-3 (single user eBook)
ISBN 978-1-4896-4042-0 (multi-user eBook)

Printed in the United States of America in Brainerd, Minnesota
1 2 3 4 5 6 7 8 9 0 19 18 17 16 15

052015
052215

Photo Credits

The publisher gratefully acknowledges the photo suppliers for this title: Getty Images, page 1; iStock, page 5; Alex Ringer, Israel, page 6; Cailan Burns, pages 7, 10, 11; Israel Talby, pages 9b, 12; Rob Friedman, page 17b; IndianSummer, page 19; Photodisc, page 20; Nancie Louie, page 21; Joy Powers, page 23; Andrei Tchernov, page 27; Howard Sandler, page 28; Sandra O'Claire, page 29. All other photographs and illustrations are © copyright UC Publishing Pty Ltd.

Every reasonable effort has been made to trace ownership and to obtain permission to reprint copyright material. The publishers would be pleased to have any errors or omissions brought to their attention so that they may be corrected in subsequent printings.

First published in 2006 by Blake Publishing
Copyright © 2006 Blake Publishing

Contents

AV² Book Code 2

What Is Judaism? 4

What Do Jewish People Believe? 7

What Is the Torah? 9

The Story of Moses 10

Prayer 12

Where Do Jewish People Worship? 13

Inside a Synagogue 14

The Rabbi 16

Special Clothes for Worship 17

The Star of David 18

The Menorah 19

Life Events 20

Keeping Kosher 24

Shabbat 25

Passover 26

Other Celebrations 28

Key Words 30

Index 31

Log on to www.av2books.com 32

What Is Judaism?

Judaism is a religion that began about 4,000 years ago in the Middle East. People who follow Judaism are called Jewish.

Over the centuries, many Jewish people have settled in different countries around the world. Today, there are Jewish people living in over 100 countries.

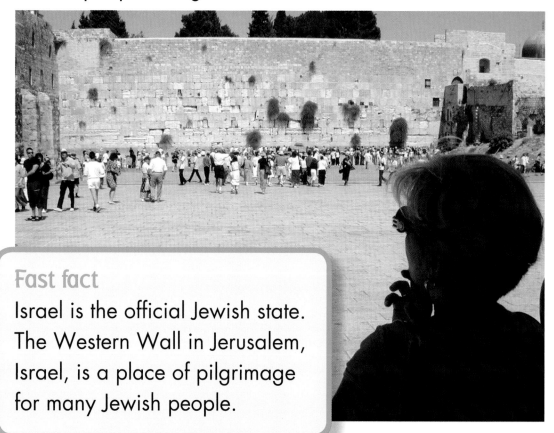

Fast fact
Israel is the official Jewish state. The Western Wall in Jerusalem, Israel, is a place of pilgrimage for many Jewish people.

The holy books of Judaism are sometimes kept in ornate cases made of precious metals. Jewish people believe the word of God is written in these books.

Jewish people have many customs and traditions.

Their customs, traditions and festivals teach them about their history and their beliefs.

However, although the followers of Judaism share the most important beliefs, they do not agree about everything.

Fast fact

At Sukkot, an important Jewish festival, people use four types of plants to celebrate the holiday. At this time, Jewish people give thanks for all things that grow and remember the difficult escape from Egypt by Jews in Biblical times.

What Do Jewish People Believe?

Jewish people believe that there is one God, who made the world and everything in it. They believe that God has existed forever and will never die.

Fast fact

An important person in Jewish history is Abraham. Abraham lived about 4,000 years ago in a city called Ur, located in modern Iraq. Abraham believed that there was only one God. He believed that God wanted him to leave his home and become the father of a great nation.

Jewish people believe they must love and worship God. They show their love by following God's teachings on how to live and behave.

Some Jewish people believe they are expected to strictly follow the teachings, or laws, of the **Torah**. The Torah is the main Jewish holy book.

Other Jewish people believe that Judaism can change to suit different times and circumstances. They believe that some of the laws of the Torah can be changed if they are no longer appropriate.

What Is the Torah?

The Torah is the first five books of the Hebrew bible. It is the holiest book in Jewish life.

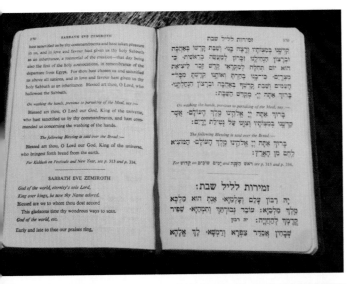

Some Jewish people believe that God gave the Torah to Moses, an important Jewish leader, about 3500 BC.

Jewish people believe that the Torah contains instructions about how God wants them to live.

Fast fact

Another important book is the **Talmud**. This is a collection of writings about Jewish laws and teachings.

The story of Moses

Moses is a very important person in Jewish history. He lived about 3500 BC.

At about this time, the Jewish people were slaves in Egypt. Moses was asked by God to rescue them from slavery. He led the Jewish people out of Egypt. The journey out of Egypt is called the Exodus.

They later settled in a place called Canaan. This is in the area that today we call Israel. Israel is the homeland of the Jewish people.

When they left Egypt, the Jews travelled for 40 years in the wilderness. Jewish people believe that, during this time in the wilderness, God called Moses to go to Mount Sinai.

When Moses reached the top of Mount Sinai, God gave him the Jewish holy book called the Torah. The Torah contained the **Ten Commandments**. Commandments are the laws and rules to lead a good life.

Prayer

Jewish people can pray any time of the day. But there are three special times in the day when they are supposed to pray: morning, afternoon and night.

The most important prayer is called the **Shema**. Some people say the Shema when they get up in the morning and before they go to bed at night. It is recited as part of the morning and evening service in the **synagogue**, which is the Jewish place of worship.

Fast fact

Traditional Jewish homes will have a small case, called a mezuzah, attached to the doorpost. Inside the case is a copy of the Shema, written on parchment.

Where Do Jewish People Worship?

Even though they believe that God can be worshipped anywhere, Jewish people have a special place where they meet to worship and pray. This special place is called a synagogue.

The synagogue is the centre of Jewish life. People go to the synagogue to pray and to listen to Torah readings, which teach them to live and behave according to Jewish laws and traditions.

Inside a Synagogue

Synagogues can look very different from the outside. But on the inside, synagogues usually have a similar pattern and the same important objects.

One of the most important objects is the cupboard where the Torah is kept. The cupboard is called the Ark. The Ark end of the synagogue faces Jerusalem, the holy capital city of Israel.

Synagogues usually have a raised platform. There is a table on the platform where the Torah can be laid while it is being read.

In some synagogues, everyone sits together. In other synagogues, women and young children sit in one area and men sit in another.

Fast fact

Most synagogues have the first words of the Ten Commandments on a plaque above the Ark.

15

The Rabbi

Every synagogue has a **rabbi**. The word *rabbi* means master or teacher. A rabbi teaches Jewish people about their religion and helps them to learn more about the Torah.

The rabbi can lead prayers in the synagogue, and can conduct wedding and funeral services. Rabbis can also give advice to people and help them if they have problems.

Fast fact

Traditionally, only men could become rabbis. Today some Jewish groups allow women to become rabbis as well.

Special Clothes for Worship

People wear special clothes when attending synagogue as a sign of respect to God.

One piece of special clothing is a small, head covering called a **kippah** or yarmulke. Some Jewish men cover their heads all the time with a kippah.

Another special piece of clothing is the tallit. A tallit is a prayer shawl worn over clothes. The most important part of the tallit is the tassels at each end.

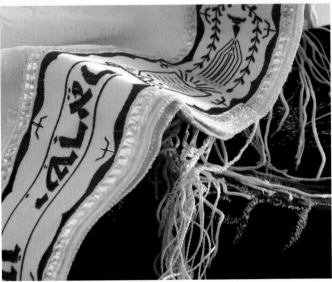

The Star of David

An important symbol for the Jewish people is the **Star of David**. The six points of the star represent the six days that God took to create the world.

The Star of David was first used years ago to represent the faith and identity of the Jewish community. The six-pointed star is now used on the national flag of the State of Israel.

Fast facts

- David was a king of ancient Israel. He is a very important figure in Jewish history.

- Jewish lore links the Star of David symbol to a shield owned by King David that protected him from enemies.

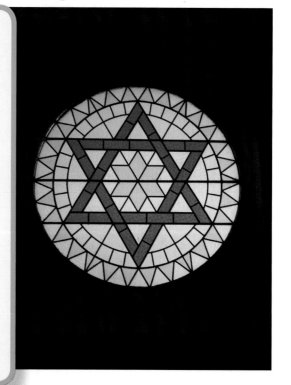

The Menorah

The seven-branched **menorah** is another very important symbol for the Jewish people. The seven branches may represent the days of the week.

The menorah has been used for centuries by Jewish people. Many centuries ago, a menorah was constantly kept burning in the temple in Jerusalem. Now it is used all over the world as a symbol for Jewish faith.

Life Events

Major life events, like births, weddings and deaths, are important religious occasions for many Jewish people. These are times when family and friends come together for special ceremonies.

These ceremonies continue Jewish traditions and customs and bring the Jewish community together. They are occasions to remember and thank God.

Bar mitzvah

For Jewish boys, their thirteenth birthday is one of the most important events in their lives. When a Jewish boy turns thirteen he celebrates his **bar mitzvah**.

That means he is considered old enough to make many decisions for himself. He becomes responsible for his actions and he also takes on obligations.

There is a ceremony in the synagogue where the boy reads parts of the Torah and sings from the holy books. After the synagogue, he goes home with his family for a feast. This is a very happy occasion and the boy receives presents from everyone.

Fast fact

There is a similar ceremony for girls. It is called a **bat mitzvah**.

Marriage

Jewish people are expected to get married and to marry a person who is also Jewish. Jewish marriages usually take place in a synagogue. A rabbi conducts the ceremony.

At the wedding, the couple stand underneath a huppah. A huppah is special canopy. This symbolizes the house they will live in together.

Death

Jewish people believe that a funeral should happen very soon after a person has died, usually within three days.

From the time the person has died to the time of burial, the body is never left on its own. A special candle is lit and placed next to the body as a sign of respect.

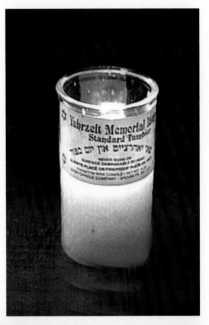

It is the custom to light a candle each year on the date of the person's death as a memorial. This candle burns for 24 hours and is called a yahrzeit.

Keeping Kosher

Jewish people have rules that tell them what food they can eat and how they should prepare it.

The word **kosher** is used to describe food that fits all the rules and that Jewish people are allowed to eat.

Many people buy their food from kosher shops. The food has labels on the packaging that guarantee it is kosher.

Shabbat

Shabbat is the Hebrew name for the Sabbath – the Jewish day of rest and worship. It begins at sunset on Friday and lasts until sunset on Saturday.

During Shabbat, people are expected to rest and do no work. This is to remember how God made the world in six days and rested on the seventh.

On Friday evening, there is a service at the synagogue. Afterwards, families get together for the most important meal of the week.

Passover

Jewish people celebrate many holy days and festivals throughout the year. **Passover** is one of the most important Jewish festivals.

It celebrates the time when the Jewish people left Egypt and were freed from slavery.

The first night of Passover is called Seder night. The family gathers for the **Seder meal**. The food and drink at the Seder meal reminds people of the escape from Egypt.

Fast fact
Jewish festivals begin in the evening and end at sunset the next day.

Charoset is a mixture of fruit and wine which looks like cement. It reminds people of the cities built by Jewish slaves in Egypt.

Matzo bread and bitter herbs remind Jews of the suffering in Egypt.

Lettuce reminds them of spring.

The egg is a symbol of new life.

Cups of wine remind them of freedom.

Other Celebrations

The most solemn Jewish festivals are Rosh Hashana (Jewish New Year) and **Yom Kippur**, which is ten days later.

The Jewish New Year, Rosh Hashana, is sometimes called the Feast of the Trumpets. It celebrates the creation of the world. It is a solemn occasion but also a time of hope.

Yom Kippur is a special day when Jewish people ask God to forgive them for all the things they have done wrong. On this day Jewish people do not work, eat or drink. They usually spend the day in prayer and meditation.

Fast fact
The shofar, a musical instrument made from a ram's horn, is used on important Jewish religious occasions. It is used at Rosh Hashana, and on Yom Kippur.

Hanukkah, the Festival of Lights, lasts for eight nights. It is a festival that celebrates freedom.

A special menorah called a hanukiah is used for this festival. The hanukiah holds eight candles plus another one called the servant candle.

Each night of Hanukkah, a candle on the hanukiah is lit. The servant candle is used to light the other candles and is lit on the first night. By the end of the festival, all the lights on the candlestick are brightly burning.

Fast fact
A popular game to play at Hanukkah is the **dreidel** game. A dreidel is like a spinning top with four flat sides. On each side is a Hebrew letter.

Key Words

bar mitzvah a Jewish celebration for a boy when he becomes 13 years old and is accepted into the congregation

bat mitzvah a Jewish celebration for a girl when she becomes 12 years old and is accepted into the congregation

dreidel a type of spinning top with four flat sides

Hanukkah a celebrations of freedom, also known as the Festival of Lights

kippah small, head covering worn by males (also called a yarmulke)

kosher food that Jewish people are allowed to eat

menorah a seven-branched candlestick; a special Jewish symbol

Passover an important Jewish festival, celebrating the journey from Egypt and freedom from slavery

rabbi Jewish religious leader

Seder meal ceremonial dinner on the first night of Passover

Shema important Jewish prayer

Star of David a special Jewish symbol in the shape of a six-pointed star

synagogue a building or meeting place for Jewish worship

Talmud collection of writings about Jewish laws and teachings

Ten Commandments ten laws given to Moses by God

Torah the first five books of the Hebrew bible

Yom Kippur an important holy day, also known as the Day of Atonement

Index

Abraham   7

beliefs   6, 7, 8, 9, 10, 11, 13

ceremonies   20, 21, 22, 24

festivals   6, 26, 28, 29

food   24, 26, 27

Moses   9, 10, 11

prayer   12, 13, 16, 28

rabbi   16, 22

special clothes   17

symbols   18, 19, 29

synagogues   12, 13, 14, 15, 16, 17, 21, 22, 25

Torah   8, 9, 11, 13, 14, 15, 16, 21

Log on to www.av2books.com

AV² by Weigl brings you media enhanced books that support active learning. Go to www.av2books.com, and enter the special code found on page 2 of this book. You will gain access to enriched and enhanced content that supplements and complements this book. Content includes video, audio, weblinks, quizzes, a slide show, and activities.

AV² Online Navigation

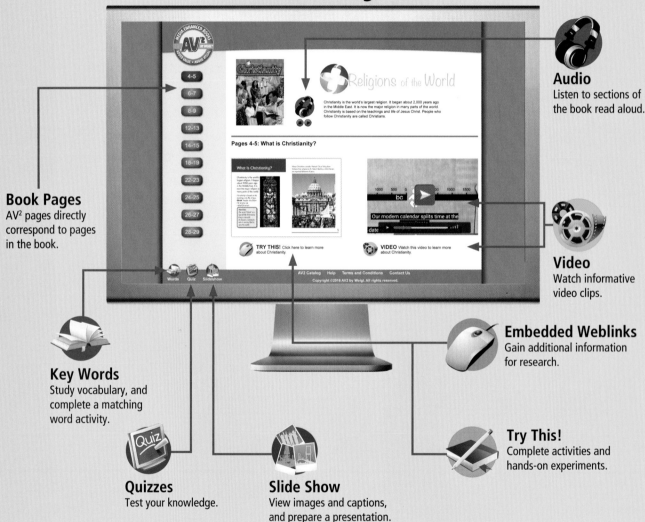

Audio
Listen to sections of the book read aloud.

Book Pages
AV² pages directly correspond to pages in the book.

Video
Watch informative video clips.

Key Words
Study vocabulary, and complete a matching word activity.

Embedded Weblinks
Gain additional information for research.

Quizzes
Test your knowledge.

Slide Show
View images and captions, and prepare a presentation.

Try This!
Complete activities and hands-on experiments.

AV² was built to bridge the gap between print and digital. We encourage you to tell us what you like and what you want to see in the future.

Sign up to be an AV² Ambassador at www.av2books.com/ambassador.

Due to the dynamic nature of the Internet, some of the URLs and activities provided as part of AV² by Weigl may have changed or ceased to exist. AV² by Weigl accepts no responsibility for any such changes. All media enhanced books are regularly monitored to update addresses and sites in a timely manner. Contact AV² by Weigl at 1-866-649-3445 or av2books@weigl.com with any questions, comments, or feedback.